Food and Recipes of the Civil War

George Erdosh

The Rosen Publishing Group's
PowerKids Press™
New York

The recipes in this cookbook are intended for a child to make together with an adult.

Many thanks to Ruth Rosen and her test kitchen.

Published in 1997 by The Rosen Publishing Group, Inc.
29 East 21st Street, New York, NY 10010

First Edition

Book Design: Danielle Primiceri

Photo Credits: Cover (left) © Corbis-Bettmann, (right) © Mark Scott/FPG International; pp. 4, 11, 13, 17, 18 (middle), 20 (top) © Archive Photos; pp. 6 (top, middle), 14 © Corbis-Bettmann; p. 6 (middle) © Jonathan Meyers/FPG International; p. 6 (bottom) © T. del/Amo/ H. Armstrong Roberts; p. 8 (middle) © PhotoDisc; p. 18 (top) © Corbis-Bettmann; p. 20 (middle) © UPI/Corbis-Bettmann.

Photo Illustrations: pp. 7, 9, 19 by Christine Innamorato and Olga Vega; pp. 8 (bottom), 18 (middle, bottom), 20 (middle, bottom) by Ira Fox.

Erdosh, George, 1935–
    Food and recipes of the Civil War / George Erdosh.
        p.   cm. — (Cooking throughout American history)
    Includes index.
    Summary: Briefly describes some of the foods eaten in the North and South before and after the Civil War and the impact of the war on what foods were available and how they were prepared. Includes recipes.
    ISBN 0-8239-5112-X
    1. Cookery, American—History—Juvenile literature. 2. United States—History—Civil War, 1861–1865—Juvenile literature. [Cookery, American—History. 2. United States—History—Civil War, 1861–1865.] I. Title. II. Series.
TX715.E657 1997
641.5973'09'034—dc21   97-20668
                                                                                              CIP
                                                                                               AC

Manufactured in the United States of America

Contents

The American Civil War

Abigail was eight years old when the American Civil War began in 1861. She and her family lived in South Carolina on a large farm called a **plantation** (plan-TAY-shun). Until the Civil War, most people in the South had plenty of food to eat. Some of the food was grown in the South. But much of the food was brought there from the North. The Civil War changed all that.

A civil war is when groups of people in the same country fight each other. The American Civil War was between the Northern states and Southern states. It lasted for four years, from April 12, 1861 to April 9, 1865.

◀ *During the four years of the American Civil War, the United States was divided into North and South. Families who lived in the North and the South fought against each other.*

Life in the South

Before the war, many people in the South had plantations. Some people grew food crops, such as rice. But most people grew cotton and tobacco because they sold for more money. These crops were sold to the Northern states and to other countries.

Many plantation owners had **slaves** (SLAYVZ) who worked in the fields. Under the unfair system of slavery, people were brought to the United States from Africa. They were not paid for their work. They were "owned" by their masters. When slaves had children, those children also became the property of their masters. It was cheaper for the plantation owners to have slaves than to pay people to work on the plantations.

Abigail was friends with a slave girl named Mary. Mary showed Abigail how to cook a type of bread called hoe cake.

Hoe Cake

You will need:

½ cup cornmeal

¼ teaspoon salt

1 ½ teaspoons
        vegetable oil

½ cup boiling water

Hoe cake was a type of bread that slaves cooked on a tool called a hoe. Hoe cake was cooked over a small fire at lunchtime.

HOW TO DO IT:

☞ Preheat the oven to 375° F.

☞ Mix cornmeal and salt in a small bowl.

☞ Add the vegetable oil and ¼ cup of the boiling water and stir well.

☞ Keep adding more water until the dough is thick and you can work it with your hands.

☞ Oil the surface of a small cookie sheet with ½ teaspoon of vegetable oil.

☞ Shape the dough by hand into two flat, round patties. Place them on the cookie sheet and put them in the oven.

☞ Bake the hoe cakes for 25 minutes, or until they are brown.

☞ Serve with butter, jam, or anything else you like on bread.

This serves two people.

Southern Cooking

Before the Civil War, Abigail's mother cooked large meals of baked or boiled meat and vegetables. The meat had lots of fat on it, and the vegetables were cooked until they were mushy. Sometimes Abigail's mother fried foods in animal fat or butter. Like most people at that time, Abigail's family seasoned their food with salt and pepper.

Abigail liked the sweets best of all. She helped her mother bake cookies, pies, and cakes. They used spices such as cinnamon, cloves, mace, ginger, and nutmeg. During the summer, they made jams and jellies. In the fall, after the pecans were harvested, Abigail's mother made **praline** (PRAY-leen) sauce. Abigail's family ate praline sauce with fruit or cake. Abigail felt lucky to be able to eat so many delicious foods.

Praline Sauce

1 cup corn syrup

3 tablespoons brown sugar

2 tablespoons water

½ cup pecans, chopped

½ teaspoon vanilla extract

HOW TO DO IT:

☞ Mix the corn syrup, brown sugar, and water in a medium-size pot.

☞ Cook it over medium heat and stir with a spoon.

☞ When it starts to boil, take the pot off the heat and stir in the pecans and vanilla extract.

☞ Serve warm over ice cream, fruit, or cake.

This makes 1½ cups of sauce and serves about four people.

Life in the North

People in the North did not agree with slavery. They were building **factories** (FAK-ter-eez) and using machines that worked faster than people could. One such machine was called a **mechanical harvester** (meh-KAN-ih-kul HAR-ves-ter). This machine picked crops, such as grain, five times faster than people could.

The North wanted to stop slavery and build more factories and better machines. But the South wanted slavery to keep their farms going. So the South separated from the North and formed its own country called the **Confederate** (kun-FED-er-et) States of America, or the **Confederacy** (kun-FED-er-uh-see). The Northern states were called the **Union** (YOON-yun).

The people of the North were better prepared to fight a war. They had machines to harvest their crops while they were fighting. They also had factories in which weapons could be made quickly. These women are making bullets in a factory in the North.

The Beginning of the Civil War

President Abraham Lincoln and people in the North wanted to keep the Northern and Southern states united. But people in the South wanted the Confederacy to be its own country. So President Lincoln declared war.

When the war started, Abigail's father joined the Confederate Army. He said that if the Union won, Abigail's family would lose their slaves and their plantation.

Abigail's cousin Thomas lived in Pennsylvania, a state in the North. Thomas's father joined the Union Army. He wanted to end slavery and to help keep the North and the South together.

President Lincoln wanted to keep the United States together, and was willing to go to war to do it. The president is shown here with Union troops. ▶

Wartime Food in the South

The four years of the Civil War were hard on the people of the South. Like Abigail's father, most men volunteered to fight for the Confederate Army. Few people were left to guard or run the cities and plantations. The North stopped shipping food to the South. Union troops stormed through the South, taking the food and **supplies** (suh-PLYZ) they needed. Many buildings and farms were destroyed. Food was hard to find.

Roads and railroads were not very good in the South. Even when there was enough food for the Confederate soldiers, it was hard to get it to them on the battlefields. Finally, starving Confederate soldiers took whatever food the Union soldiers had left. Many Southerners, plantation owners and slaves alike, were left without enough to eat.

◀ *Union troops sometimes burned down Southern towns and plantations, leaving families homeless and hungry. This picture was taken in Richmond, Virginia in April 1865.*

Wartime Food in the North

People in the North, like Abigail's cousin Thomas, hardly felt the effects of the war. Thomas's family always had plenty of food to eat. They had to pay a little more for it, and sometimes they couldn't buy some of the things they wanted, but few people went hungry.

The Union Army soldiers of the North had plenty to eat during battles with the Confederates. **Engineers** (en-jin-EERZ) built new roads and railroads to carry food to the Union soldiers wherever they were. Other engineers created machines that made ice. Ice kept meat cold while it was shipped to the soldiers. Still other engineers built bigger and better boats to carry more food and weapons to the Union soldiers.

The Union soldiers had more food and better weapons so they were ▶
able to fight longer and harder than the Confederate soldiers.

What Did the Soldiers Eat?

Each Union Army soldier received a lot of food every day—a big piece of meat; a loaf of bread; butter; dried beans, peas, rice, or **hominy** (HAH-min-ee); coffee or tea; sugar and molasses; and salt and pepper. The Union Army often had kitchens set up on the battlefields and cooks who prepared food for the soldiers.

Northern factories began to produce canned milk and juice, which also was sent to the soldiers. A company in California started to can fruits and vegetables. Soon Union soldiers were able to buy canned meat and fish as well.

Confederate Army soldiers received only a small piece of pork, bacon, or beef every few days, and cornbread or a dry, tasteless cracker called hardtack. The Confederate Army soldiers had to cook for themselves most of the time.

Salt Pork in Cornmeal Coat

½ pound salt pork
¼ cup cornmeal
½ cup vegetable oil

HOW TO DO IT:

☞ Ask an adult to help you cut the skin off the salt pork. Cut the salt pork into thick slices.

☞ Put the slices into a small pot and cover them with water. Heat the pot on medium heat until the water starts to boil.

☞ Turn the heat off and let the salt pork sit in the hot water for five minutes. Drain the water.

☞ When the salt pork cools, spread the cornmeal on a large plate. Dip the salt pork slices into the cornmeal, coating the slices on both sides. Shake off the extra cornmeal.

☞ Heat vegetable oil in a heavy pan on medium heat. When the oil is hot, gently slip the coated salt pork slices into the oil. Brown them on both sides, about five minutes on each side.

This serves four to five people.

The South Is in Trouble

By the end of the war, food **shortages** (SHOR-tej-ez) were common in the South. Like many people, Abigail and her mother were starving. They and the slaves often ate only one meal a day. Basic foods, such as flour and cornmeal, were very **expensive** (ex-PEN-siv). There was no coffee or sugar. It was hard to keep meat from spoiling. The trains that once brought ice to different parts of the South had stopped running. And there was not enough salt to **preserve** (pre-ZERV) the meat.

By 1863, there was so little food that Abigail's mother and many other women started food **riots** (RY-ets) to get the attention of the government. But the government was helpless—there just was not enough food for anyone. Abigail often dreamed of the food she would eat when the war was over.

Sweet Potato Pie

You will need:

1 pound sweet
 potatoes
2 eggs
1¼ cups milk
¾ cup brown sugar
½ teaspoon salt
1 teaspoon cinnamon
½ teaspoon nutmeg
3 tablespoons butter,
 melted
1 9-inch pie crust

HOW TO DO IT:

☞ Preheat the oven to 425° F.
☞ Peel, wash, and cut the sweet potatoes into 1-inch pieces.
☞ Put enough water in a medium-size pot to cover the sweet potatoes and add ½ teaspoon salt.
☞ Bring the water to boil, then turn the heat to low. Cover the pot and let the sweet potatoes simmer for 20 minutes until soft.
☞ Drain the water and mash the sweet potatoes in a large bowl.
☞ Beat the eggs in a small bowl with a fork. Add eggs, milk, brown sugar, salt, cinnamon, nutmeg, and melted butter to sweet potatoes. Mix well and pour into the pie crust.
☞ Bake the pie at 425° F for 10 minutes. Then turn the heat down to 300° F and bake for 50 minutes.
This serves six to eight people.

Food After the War

When the war finally ended, the North and South were united once again. The slaves were set free. Some went north to find work and housing. Other freed slaves stayed in the South. Southern families that had once been wealthy were now poor. They needed to find work and housing too.

Many people in the North and the South worked hard to help rebuild the South. The North began sending food to the South again. Abigail's mother stocked her kitchen with many different kinds of tinned, or canned, food. Abigail liked sweetened **condensed** (kun-DENST) milk the best.

The Civil War was hard on many people, and the country saw many changes. Two great ways of preserving food were developed: canning and freezing foods or cooling them with ice made by machines. These new ways of preserving food helped Americans improve the quality of the food they ate.

Glossary

condensed (kun-DENST) Reduced to a smaller form.

Confederacy (kun-FED-er-uh-see) Another name for the group of eleven Southern states that left the United States.

confederate (kun-FED-er-et) A group that is united for a purpose.

engineer (en-jin-EER) A person who designs or builds things.

expensive (ex-PEN-siv) Costing a lot of money.

factory (FAK-ter-ee) A building in which things are made by machines.

hominy (HAH-min-ee) Corn that has no hull and is white in color.

mechanical harvester (meh-KAN-ih-kul HAR-ves-ter) A machine that picks crops.

praline (PRAY-leen) A candy or sauce that is made from pecans and brown sugar.

plantation (plan-TAY-shun) A large farm on which crops such as cotton, tobacco, sugarcane, and rubber trees are grown.

preserve (pre-ZERV) To keep food from spoiling.

riot (RY-et) A noisy protest of people against something they don't like.

shortage (SHOR-tej) A time during which there is not enough of some things.

slave (SLAYV) A person who is "owned" by another person.

supplies (suh-PLYZ) The food and equipment necessary for an army to live and fight.

Union (YOON-yun) The Northern states during the American Civil War.

Index

DATE DUE
